C[illegible]S CAROL

CHARLES DICKENS

2005, licensed for:
Bildungshaus Schulbuchverlage
Westermann Schroedel Diesterweg
Schönigh Winklers GmbH
Georg-Westermann-Allee 66
38104 Braunschweig
Germany

This edition published by Richmond Publishing® 2006

ISBN:84-668-0817-5
ISBN:3-425-71904-1

Printed in Italy by Techno Media Reference

Adaptation, exercises and notes: Barbara Chatwin

Language Consultant: Gabrielle Hodson-Hirst

Illustrations: Philip Norton

Richmond PUBLISHING

Diesterweg®

A Christmas Carol

A young man walked into an office in London. Over the door were the words SCROOGE AND MARLEY. Mr. Scrooge was the young man's uncle. Everybody [1] in London knew Mr. Scrooge. He was very rich but also very mean [2]. The most important thing in his life was money! Mr. Marley was dead. "Good morning Uncle. Merry [3] Christmas." "Pardon? Did you say Merry Christmas?" "Yes, Uncle, I did. Tomorrow is Christmas Day." "I don't like Christmas," said SCROOGE, "people spend money at Christmas. I hate [4] spending [5] money!"

1. **everybody:** all the people.
2. **mean:** never kind.
3. **merry:** happy.
4. **to hate:** is the opposite of *to love*.
5. **to spend:** to pay to buy things.

ACTIVITY

**How much English do you know?
Look at the numbers and write
a word in the column.**

1	2	3	4	5	6	7	8	9	10	11	12	13	14
M	E	R	R	Y	C	H	R	I	S	T	M	A	Ş

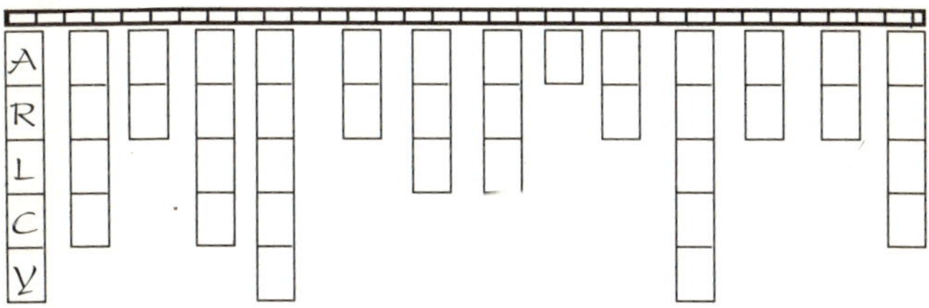

1. A person

2. A number

3. A colour

4. Opposite of left

5. A colour

6. An animal

7. Opposite of love

8. Opposite of poor

9. A preposition

10. Past of sit

11. A number

12. Plural of man

13. Verb: to be

14. Verb: using money

"Come and have dinner with us tomorrow," said Scrooge's nephew[1]. "No," Scrooge answered. "But it's Christmas," insisted the young man. "No. I will not pass the day singing and dancing like an idiot," said Scrooge. "Very well, Uncle," and the young man went out. In the corner of the office there was a man working. This was Bob Cratchit, Mr. Scrooge's clerk[2]. Bob Cratchit was a very nice[3] person. He had a big family and he worked very hard[4] for Mr. Scrooge for little money. He was very cold because old Scrooge never bought much wood for the fire. He was wearing a coat, a scarf and a pair of gloves[5]!

1. **nephew:** a brother's son.
2. **clerk:** a person who works in an office.
3. **nice:** pleasant/good.
4. **to work hard:** to work a lot.
5. **coat, scarf, gloves:** clothes.

ACTIVITY

What was Bob Cratchit wearing in the office?

a coat **a hat** **a scarf** **a jacket** **gloves**

He was wearing a coat.

He wasn't ....

He ....

....

What are you wearing?
Write four sentences.

....

....

....

....

At six o'clock Bob Cratchit went to Mr. Scrooge. "Excuse me, sir. Tomorrow is Christmas Day, can I stay at home?" "Stay at home," shouted Scrooge. "I don't pay [1] you to stay at home!" "But it is Christmas," said Cratchit. "Very well," said Scrooge, "but you must work double hours on Boxing Day [2]!" "Yes sir, certainly sir, Merry Christmas, sir." "Get out [3]," shouted Scrooge. "Christmas! Everybody talks about Christmas!" said Scrooge. "It's just [4] an excuse not to work. People want money too. Always money! For doing nothing!" Scrooge put on his hat and coat and left the office.

1. **to pay:** to give money for working.
2. **Boxing Day:** 26th of December.
3. **to get out:** to go out of the office.
4. **just:** only.

ACTIVITY

On Christmas Eve, I go shopping.

On Christmas Day, I have dinner at home.

On Boxing Day, I go for a walk.

✎ **What do you do at Christmas? Draw the pictures and write the sentences.**

.... Eve	.... Day	.... Day
....	....	....
....	....	....
....	....	....

It was Christmas Eve and everyone was shopping. They bought decorations[1] for the tree and things to eat.
On his way home, Scrooge met[2] two men.
"Good evening, Mr. Scrooge. Can you give some money for the poor[3] people?"
"No," said Scrooge.
"But it's Christmas," said the men.
"I have no money to give people who don't want to work," said Scrooge. "At Christmas or at any other time. Good evening, gentlemen."
They watched Scrooge walk away.
"It's terrible." said the men "Scrooge has so much money but he never helps the poor."

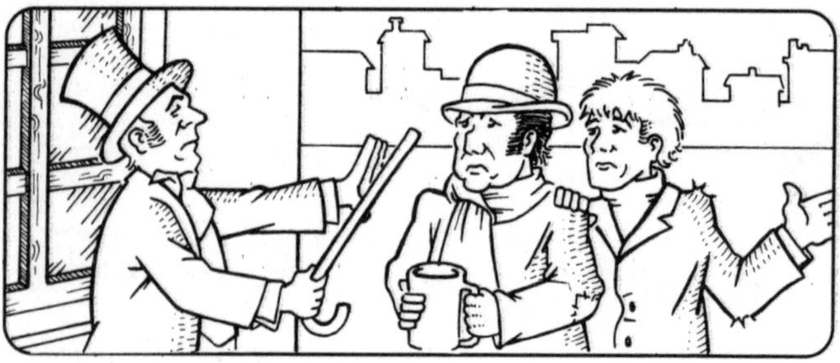

1. **decorations:** pretty things to put on the Christmas tree.
2. **met:** is the past tense of *to meet*; to see and to speak to someone.
3. **poor:** people with no money.

ACTIVITY

Look at the examples.
Write sentences for the pictures.

He is on his way to work.

He is coming back from work.

Now write the sentences for these pictures.

.... the cinema.

.... the park.

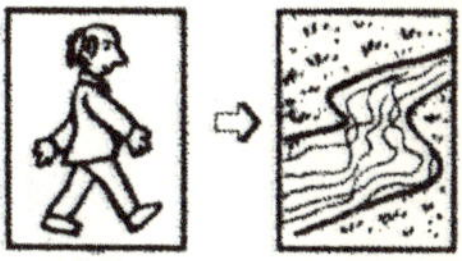

.... the river.

.... the mountains.

It was snowing [1] and almost dark [2] when Scrooge arrived home. He took his key out of his pocket to open the door, and stopped! On the door was a face. It was Marley's face! The man who worked with him and now was dead. The face was very white and the eyes stared [3] at Scrooge, then it disappeared.
"Oh dear," thought Scrooge.
"I am very tired [4]."
In the house Scrooge locked [5] the door once, twice, three times! Scrooge kept all his money in the house. Under the mattress [6]. He didn't believe in banks.

1. **to snow:** it snows when it's very cold.
2. **dark:** no light.
3. **to stare:** to look at continuously.
4. **tired:** you want to sleep.
5. **to lock:** to close a door with a key.
6. **mattress:** you sleep on one.

ACTIVITY

Look at the diagram and the example.

I go to the
- PARK
- CINEMA
- MOUNTAINS
- SEA

Once .... = one time
Twice .... = two times
.... = three times

- a day
- a week
- a month
- a year

I go to the park **once a day**.

Now write sentences using the indications above.

....

....

....

....

Now write the sentences in the negative.

....

....

....

....

Mr. Scrooge sat down to eat his soup. Then, he heard a noise[1]. A terrible noise! The door opened. Scrooge was petrified[2]. There was Marley! He had chains on his feet and on his arms.

"Is that you, Marley?" asked Scrooge. "What do you want? Why are you here?"

"I want to help you," said Marley.

"I need no help from you," answered Scrooge.

"You must do as I say," said the ghost. "I visit many people I knew when I was alive[3]. I must help them or I will have these chains for eternity.

Three Spirits will visit you tonight. The first one will come at one o'clock. You must be ready[4]!"

Marley's ghost went out of the window.

1. **noise:** sound.
2. **to be petrified:** to be afraid.
3. **alive:** is the opposite of *dead*.
4. **to be ready:** to be prepared.

ACTIVITY

Draw the picture of Marley and Scrooge, as you imagine it from the story.

chains

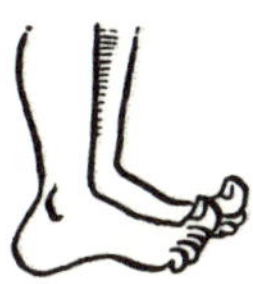

feet

arms

one o'clock

Scrooge went to sleep, but at one o'clock he woke[1] up. Near the end of the bed was a man! Scrooge was very frightened.
"Who are you? What do you want?"
"I am the Spirit of Christmas Past. YOUR past, Scrooge. Now come with me."
"No thank you," said Scrooge. "It's very cold outside[2]."
"Do you remember your friend Marley?" asked the Spirit. "Of course, I do. He was here a few[3] hours ago."
"Well, if you don't come with me you will be like[4] him when you are dead," said the Spirit. "Close your eyes."
"I am dreaming[5]," said Scrooge and closed his eyes.

1. **woke:** is the past tense of *to wake*; to stop sleeping.
2. **outside:** not in the house.
3. **a few:** a small number, 3 or 4.
4. **to be like:** to be similar.
5. **to dream:** when you sleep you sometimes dream.

WHAT'S THE TIME?

It's one o'clock.

It's a quarter past one.

It's half past one.

It's a quarter to 3.

Write the times.

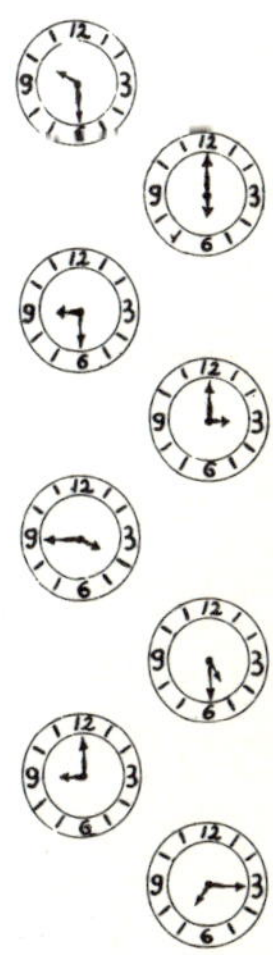

....

....

....

....

....

....

....

....

"Open your eyes," said the Spirit.
"Oh dear," said Scrooge, "are you still here?"
"Do you know this town?" asked the Spirit.
"Of course,[1] I do, I lived here. Look, there's the butcher[2]. It's Christmas. Look at all those turkeys[3]. And there's Mr. Brown the baker[4]."
"Yes," said the Spirit. "It's another Christmas." Now they were in a school room. In a corner there was one boy alone. All the other children were at home for Christmas. "Do you know that boy over there with no friends?"
"Yes, that was me. I was always alone[5]."

1. **of course:** naturally.
2. **butcher:** person who sells meat.
3. **turkey:** a bird we eat at Christmas.
4. **baker:** person who sells bread.
5. **alone:** no other person present.

ACTIVITY

✎ **Find ten words from the story.**

S	C	R	O	O	G	E	A	T
P	A	E	Y	E	L	R	A	M
I	T	D	E	Y	D	O	T	E
R	B	A	K	E	R	Y	O	B
I	D	F	R	I	E	N	D	K
T	N	B	U	T	C	H	E	R
C	H	R	I	S	T	M	A	S

✎ **List the words.**

Christmas ....

....

....

....

....

"There is my sister," said Scrooge. "She was the only person who visited me or loved me. She's dead. I have no family now."

"You have your sister's son, your nephew," said the Spirit.

Scrooge didn't answer.

The Spirit took[1] Scrooge to a party in a different town.

"I worked here, look, there's my dear friend Dick. We shared[2] a flat.

Hello, Dick, Hello, Mr. Fezziwig, it's me Ebenezer."

"They can't hear or see you," said the Spirit. "They are all very happy, aren't they?" said Scrooge. "We all loved Mr. Fezziwig."

"It's nice[3] to be loved, isn't it?" said the Spirit.

1. **took:** is the past tense of *to take*; to go with.
2. **to share:** to divide/to live in the same flat.
3. **nice:** pleasant.

ACTIVITY

✎ **Look at these pictures.**

nose

smell

eye

see

ear

hear

tongue

taste

✎ **Complete the sentences using one of the words above.**

This flower **smells** nice ....

This perfume .... terrible.

This bread ....

This turkey ....

I can .... music

.... chains

I can .... a beautiful picture.

.... terrible house.

What do you do with your ears?

....

What do you do with your nose?

....

What do you do with your eyes?

....

What do you do with your tongue?

....

DING, DONG, DING, DONG.
"What's that?" cried Scrooge. "The clock, it's the clock. I'm in bed. It was a dream. No, a nightmare[1]!" "No," said a voice, "not a dream." "Not again[2]," said Scrooge."Who are you?" "I am the Spirit of Christmas Present. Come with me." The spirit took Scrooge to a house. "This is Bob Cratchit's house," said Scrooge. "What a lot of children he has! That little boy is lame[3]. You are a Spirit, can't you do something?" "I can do nothing," said the Spirit. "And he will die because they haven't enough[4] money to pay a doctor." "I pay him a good salary," said Scrooge, "He can pay a doctor, can't he?" "Doctors are not expensive for you, but they are for him," answered the Spirit.

1. **nightmare:** a very bad dream.
2. **again:** another time.
3. **lame:** a person who can't walk very well.
4. **enough:** sufficient.

ACTIVITY

Answer the questions about the story.

Where is Scrooge? ....

Is Marley with Scrooge? ....

Which Spirit is present? ....

Whose house do they visit? ....

Why will the lame boy die? ....

Complete these sentences.

He has enough money.

.... time

.... work

.... books

Now write the sentences in the negative.

He hasn't enough money.

....

....

....

Mrs. Cratchit was laying the table[1] and the children were helping. The little boy was at the window. "Here's Daddy," he cried. The door opened and Bob Cratchit came in and picked[2] the little boy up. "Hello Tiny Tim, and how are you?" "I'm fine, Daddy." "Dinner's ready," called Mrs. Cratchit. "What a terrific[3] turkey," said Tiny Tim. "That's not a turkey," said Scrooge, "It's a pigeon[4]! Look how small it is!" "They have no money for a bigger turkey," said the Spirit. "Oh look," said a little girl, "Christmas pudding[5]! Is there a surprise inside?" "Of course, there is," answered her mother.

1. **to lay the table:** to put plates, glasses, etc. on the table.
2. **to pick up:** to take in your arms.
3. **terrific:** fantastic.
4. **pigeon:** a small type of bird.
5. **pudding:** a dessert, a sweet.

ACTIVITY

A big turkey

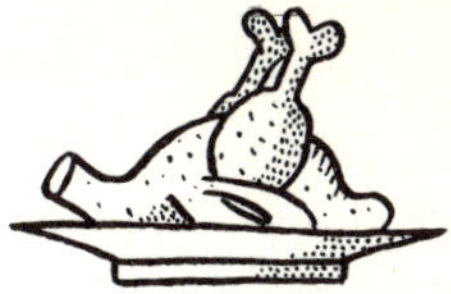

A bigger turkey

The biggest turkey

Using comparatives and superlatives write about the pictures below. Remember words ending in "Y" become "I".

Example Lucy is the *prettiest* girl in the class.

tasty pudding

small house

nice girl

big surprise

....

....

....

....

All the family sat down to dinner. The children were chatting [1].
"What a gorgeous [2] dinner," they said. "Can we start?"
"First, we will drink a toast [3] to everyone," said Bob Cratchit.
"Yes," shouted all the family. "Including Mr. Scrooge."
"No, never," said Mrs. Cratchit. "He's horrible and unkind," shouted the children. "Come, come," said Bob Cratchit, "It's Christmas." "Very well," said the family. "Merry Christmas to everyone including miserable [4] old Mr. Scrooge!"
"Charming [5] family," said Scrooge.

1. **to chatter:** to talk non-stop.
2. **gorgeous:** beautiful, magnificent.
3. **to drink a toast:** to drink to somebody on a special occasion.
4. **miserable:** unhappy.
5. **charming:** very nice.

ACTIVITY

✎ **What sort of people are they?**
Put the letters in the correct order, then put an appropriate adjective under the pictures.

GAMHRCIN-BMSREELIA-DNIKUN-RILBREOH

He's ....

He's ....

He's ....

They're ....

✎ **Write sentences like this using the words.**

Scrooge is a miserable man.

....

....

....

The Spirit took Scrooge to another[1] house. "This is my nephew's house and that's his wife. Pretty[2] woman isn't she?" "You don't know her, do you?" asked the Spirit? "No, I never go to their house for dinner." "Listen to them," said the Spirit. "I asked my uncle to come to dinner but as usual he said he was busy[3]. Busy on Christmas Day. Ridiculous[4]," said Fred, Scrooge's nephew. "I'm sorry for Uncle Scrooge," said Fred's wife. "All that money and no friends. Nobody loves him."
The Spirit and Scrooge visited many houses. Big and small houses. Rich and poor families. But in every house the people were happy!. "Stop, Stop," cried Scrooge. "I'm tired, I want to go to bed. I give my word I will think about Christmas next year. Please, take me home now. Spirit, Spirit, where are you."
The Spirit wasn't there.

1. **another:** not the same, different.
2. **pretty:** good-looking.
3. **to be busy:** to have a lot of work to do.
4. **ridiculous:** stupid.

ACTIVITY

✎ **Answer true or false.**
Put a tick in the correct box.

	T	F
Scrooge is very rich.	✔	
Scrooge was in the sitting room.		
It was Boxing Day.		
Scrooge was happy.		
It was Christmas Eve.		
Scrooge's niece was pretty.		
Scrooge always goes to dinner.		

✎ **Now write the correct sentences.**

....

....

....

....

....

....

....

It was dark and Scrooge was alone. He saw a person dressed in black[1]. "Are you the Spirit of Christmas to come?" asked Scrooge. The Spirit didn't speak. It pointed[2] to a group[3] of people. The people were talking. "Is he dead?" asked one man. "Yes. No-one will cry for him," said another. "He was a horrible, unkind man. He never gave money to us poor people. He wasn't a happy man." "Who is dead?" asked Scrooge. The Spirit pointed down. It was a grave[4]. There were no flowers and no people there. "Who is it?" asked Scrooge nervously. The Spirit pointed again. "No, I don't want to look, I want to go home." But the Spirit didn't move. Very slowly Scrooge rubbed[5] the snow away. On the grave were the words EBENEZER SCROOGE.

1. **dressed in black:** wearing black clothes.
2. **to point:** to indicate with a finger.
3. **a group:** a number.
4. **grave:** tomb where dead people are put.
5. **to rub away:** to cancel, to take away.

Which spirit is this?

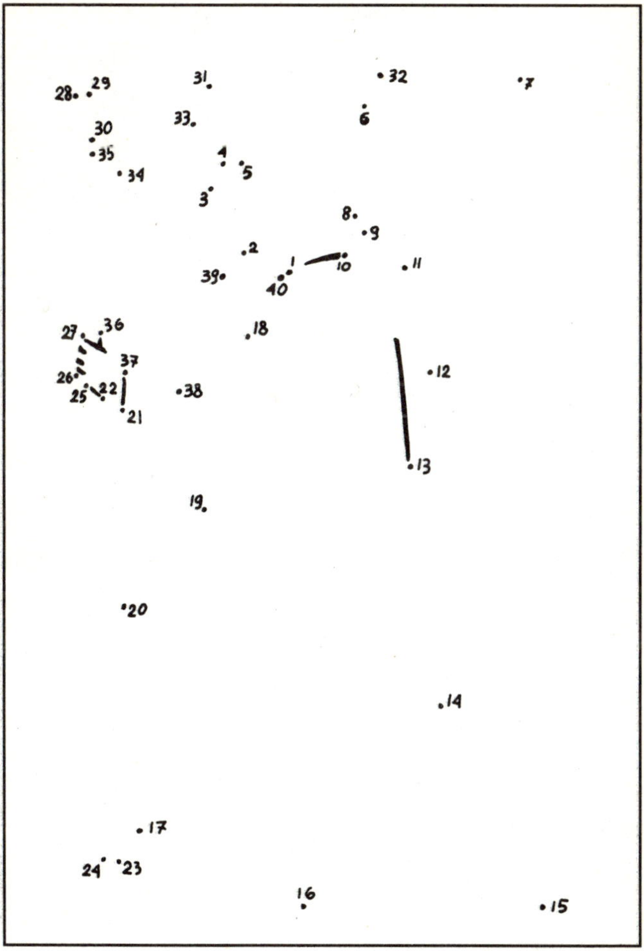

It's ....

It was morning. Christmas morning. Scrooge was in bed! "I'm alive, I'm alive[1], how wonderful!" He jumped out of bed, singing and dancing he went around the room. "What a beautiful day it is. I love Christmas. I love everybody."
He went to the butcher's and said, "Take the biggest turkey you have to Bob Cratchit's house."
He went to the florist's[2] and said, "Take these beautiful flowers to my nephew's house. They are for his wife!"
Scrooge met the two men collecting money for the poor. "Please take this," said Scrooge to the men and gave them a big sum of money for the poor. From that Christmas Scrooge was a new man[3]. He helped the poor and was kind to everyone. Bob Cratchit's son didn't die. Scrooge paid for the doctors.
Scrooge was a happy man and everybody loved him.

1. **alive:** not dead.
2. **florist:** person who sells flowers.
3. **a new man:** a different man.

ACTIVITY

**What do these shops sell?
Write the words below under the correct shop.**

butcher	baker	florist	greengrocer

....	....	....	....
....	....	....	....
....	....	....	....

roses

sausages

daffodils

cakes

strawberries

loaves

cherries

steak

iris

tomatoes

turkey

rolls

What do you like? Write sentences like this.

I like cakes but I don't like steak.

....

....

....

....

....

....

....